COMPOSER SHOWCASE

HAL LEONARD STUDENT PIANO LIBRARY

At the Lake

10 EXPRESSIVE PIANO SOLOS AND DUETS

BY ELVINA PEARCE

CONTENTS

2   *Practice and Performance Notes*

5   Sunrise Waltz

6   Sailing

9   Canoe Ride

10   Sandcastle

12   Foggy Night

14   Lighthouse

15   Beach Volleyball

18   Seagull's Lament

20   Skipping Stones

22   Drifting Clouds

Photo of Elvina Pearce by Raeleen H. Horn

ISBN 978-1-4803-9923-5

HAL•LEONARD®
CORPORATION

7777 W. BLUEMOUND RD. P.O. BOX 13819 MILWAUKEE, WI 53213

In Australia Contact:
Hal Leonard Australia Pty. Ltd.
4 Lentara Court
Cheltenham, Victoria, 3192 Australia
Email: ausadmin@halleonard.com.au

Visit Hal Leonard Online at
www.halleonard.com

Practice and Performance Notes

As a pianist, whenever I find a piece that I want to learn to play, I always search for some practice procedures that will help me learn it as quickly as possible and with a minimum amount of effort. As a teacher, I have found that my students have a similar goal for the pieces they want to learn to play.

Below are some of the practice tips I would suggest for the pieces in *At the Lake* so that you can learn them easily and enjoy creating their musical effects as soon as possible.

Sunrise Waltz

1. *Which hand has the melody?*

2. Work out the LH. (Count aloud and listen for a smooth legato.) *The RH is made of only how many different intervals?* To learn the RH quickly:

   - Circle only the changes. (C & E in m. 2; C & E♭ in m. 3; back to C & E in m. 4; C & F in m. 7, etc.)

   - Play only the RH changes. (For now, ignore the staccatos and the rhythm.)

   - When easy, play RH as written. (This time count and listen for *pp* and staccato.)

   - When secure hands separately at a super-slow tempo (♩ = 92), work on hands together. (When easy, add the dynamic changes and the *ritard*.)

Sailing

Poor pedaling in a piece can easily detract from its overall musical expression. In my studio, my students know that we never add the pedal or even discuss it until a piece can be played 100 percent securely without it. Let's suppose that "Sailing" is now ready for added pedaling. Here are my suggested practice tips for mm. 26 to the end of the piece.

1. Play LH only at a super slow tempo (♩ = 69), and count aloud.

2. Whenever the pedal must lift, <u>stop</u> and listen. *Is it clear?* If satisfied, continue on with pedal held down until the next pedal lift.

3. When playing LH only with pedal is easy, add the RH. (Be sure to continue to count and stop to listen for 100 percent clarity on each pedal lift before continuing on with the next pedaled segment.)

4. When easy, play hands together at the same very slow tempo without pausing at the pedal changes. When this is easy, gradually increase the tempo until you can play it with correct pedaling at ♩. = 72.

Canoe Ride

1. *In mm. 1–8, the LH is made of only how many different notes?*

   Play all three LH notes blocked together.

2. *In mm. 1–9, the RH is made of how many different notes?* Block them.

   - With alternating hands, play each hand blocked: LH, RH, LH, RH, etc., being sure to observe the *8va* move in mm. 5–8.

   - In mm. 9–12 practice LH moves and add the RH.

   - Play the whole piece as written. When easy, add dynamics and pedal.

Sandcastle

If we were building a sandcastle, we would first need to construct its foundation, then put up its walls, build the tower, add some arches, a tunnel, etc. When it's all built, then we can begin to decorate it – carve designs into the sand, add a drawbridge, make some windows, maybe a staircase, build a moat, etc. Building a piece is much like building a sandcastle. We first have to construct it (learn its notes, rhythm and fingering), and then when secure, we add the decorations – the dynamics, pedal, ritards and other expressive markings, etc.

As soon as "Sandcastle" is accurate and technically secure, it's ready to be decorated.

1. Circle each dynamic marking (*mp*, *pp*, etc.), and the *ritard* and *cresc.*

2. Consider the "should-sound" for each four-measure group. Then add the pedal, play the four-measure group, and <u>stop</u>. Ask yourself, "*Did my playing match my plan?*"

3. When satisfied with each shorter segment, then play whole piece. *Did you hear what you expected to hear?*

Foggy Night

Sometimes when a piece has a melody and accompaniment, it's not easy to play the accompaniment hand softer than the melody hand. *In mm. 3–15 of "Foggy Night," which hand has the melody?* Here are three practice tips for learning how to play the RH softer than the LH.

1. Work In four-measure groups. At a super-slow tempo ($\flat$ = 80) and <u>without</u> the pedal, play the LH melody very legato and with a rich, *mf* tone, and play the RH accompaniment detached and *pp*.

2. When easy, again practice in 4-measure segments, still super-slow, but now with added pedal. *Were you satisfied with the balance between the melody and the accompaniment?*

3. Now play the whole piece as written but still very slowly. When easy, gradually increase the tempo until it's easy to play it at ♩. = 66.

Lighthouse

1. *Why will the LH be easy to learn in this piece?*

2. *In mm. 3–11, how many different sized intervals are there in the RH?*

3. *How will you practice the RH in order to learn it quickly?* (See the tips for "Sunrise Waltz.")

4. *In which measures do the hands have to move either higher or lower on the keyboard?* For practicing the moves:

   • Play the RH going from mm. 6–7, and from 11–12.

   • Play the LH going from mm. 6–7 and from 9–10.

Beach Volleyball

Understanding how a piece is put together (its form) makes it easier to learn.

1. "Beach Volleyball" is a three-part piece. The first part (let's call it the A section) ends in m. 8. Enclose mm. 1–8 in parentheses and write the letter "A" above the first measure.

2. Part two (the B section) begins in m. 9. Enclose mm. 9–16 in parentheses and write the letter "B" above m. 9. *How is the B section different from A? How is it like A?*

3. *The A section returns in which measure?* Enclose mm. 17 to the end in parentheses. *Which two measures are different from the first "A" section?* Circle them. Because of this slight difference, we call this section "A prime" (A¹). Write A¹ above m. 17.

Seagull's Lament

1. *What's a "lament?"*

2. *Which player has the melody?* (Tapering the slur endings in both the primo and secondo parts helps to suggest a sighing effect in the seagull's sad song.)

3. In the primo, try these practice tips to help focus on tapering the phrase endings.

   • In m. 2, play the RH E going down to D. (*Was the D softer than the E?*)

   • In m. 1 of the RH, play just beat 3 (the E) followed by both notes in m. 2. *Was the last note soft enough to suit you?*

   • Play all of mm. 1 and 2. *What special thing will you be listening for?*

   • Still focusing on the sound of the last note of each phrase, work backwards in mm. 5–8, first playing mm. 7 and 8, then mm. 6–8, and finally, the whole phrase. *Were you satisfied with each phrase ending?*

Skipping Stones

1. *How many sections does this piece have?* (Enclose and label each of them.)

2. With a colored pen, circle the staccato dots and trace over the accent symbols in mm. 1, 2, 4, and 16–17.

   • Play just these measures, listening for crisp staccatos and strong accents.

   • Play mm. 3–4 and 3 & 5 (2nd ending), checking both the legato and staccatos.

3. Look at the LH in the primo part of the "B" section.

   • In mm. 6, 7, 9, and 10–11, play only the LH up-stem half-note slurs, listening for legato and tapered slur endings.

   • In the same measures, add the LH 5th finger whole note. Be sure to hold the whole note as you play the upper-note slurs.

Drifting Clouds

The form of this piece includes an introduction (m. 1), an ending coda (mm. 18–the end), and three main sections.

1. The "A" section begins in m. 2. *In which measure does section two (the "B" section) begin?*

2. *Is the 3rd section "A" or "A¹?"*

3. Enclose each section in parentheses and label them.

4. *What one thing will probably need the most practice in each section?*

Sunrise Waltz

By Elvina Pearce

Sailing

By Elvina Pearce

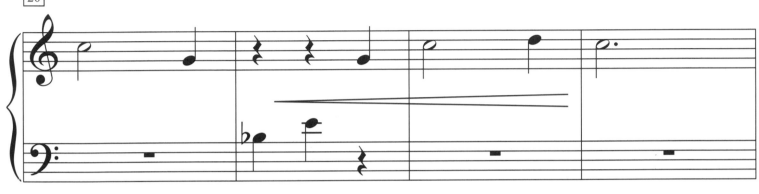

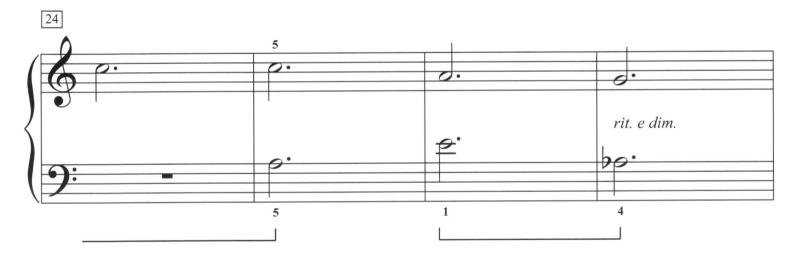

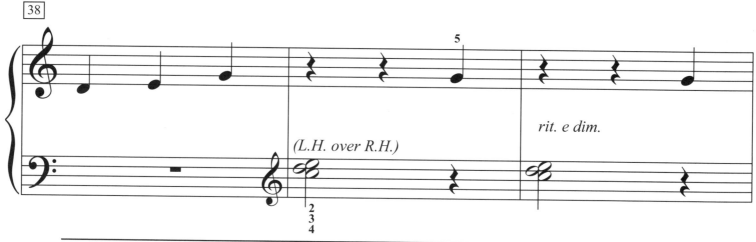

Canoe Ride

By Elvina Pearce

Sandcastle

By Elvina Pearce

Hold damper pedal down through m. 15.

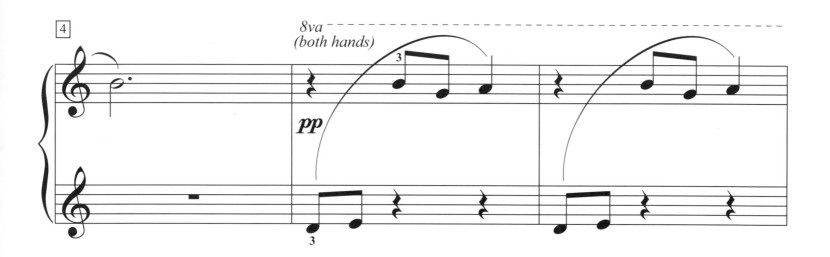

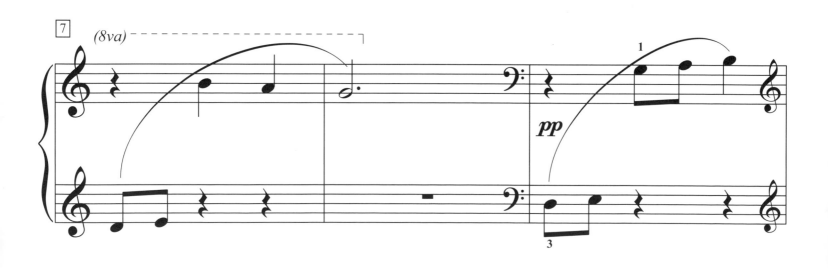

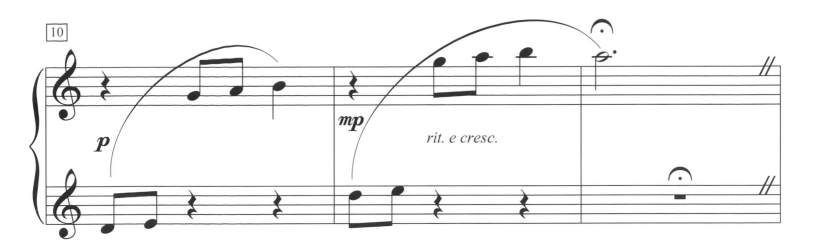

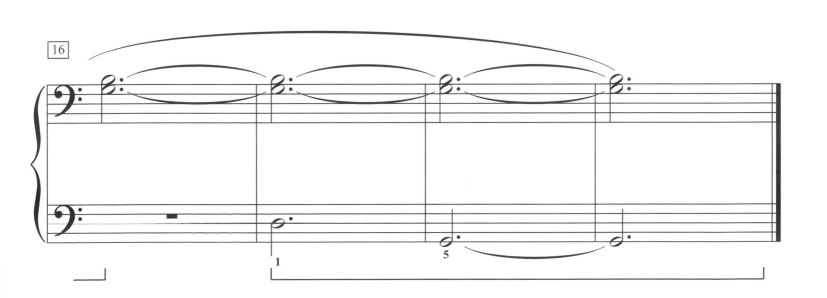

Foggy Night

By Elvina Pearce

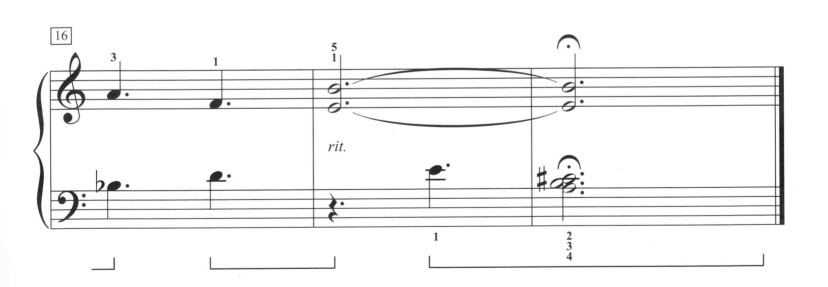

Lighthouse

By Elvina Pearce

Beach Volleyball

By Elvina Pearce

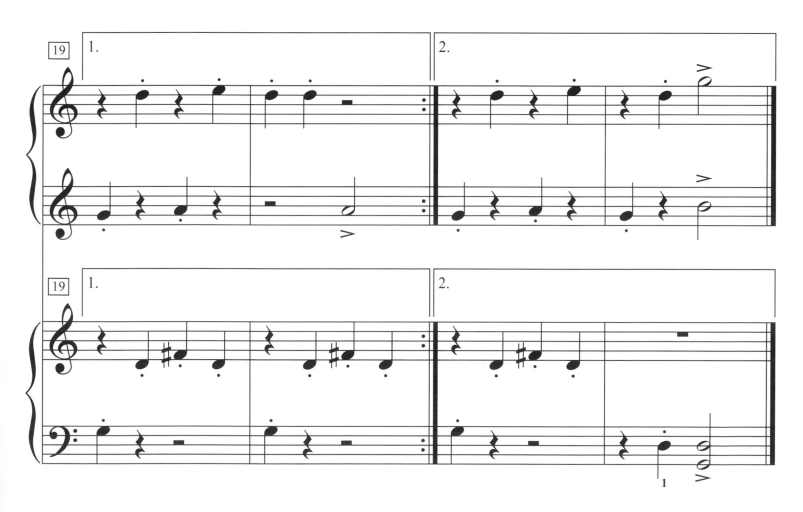

Seagull's Lament

By Elvina Pearce

Skipping Stones

By Elvina Pearce

Drifting Clouds

By Elvina Pearce